Refused a Second Date

Maya Williams

Harbor Editions
Small Harbor Publishing

Cover photo of Kimnada Bobb Jordan at church in February/March 1996,
          photographer unknown
Cover design by Allison Blevins
Book layout by Allison Blevins and Ellie Davis

REFUSED A SECOND DATE
MAYA WILLIAMS
ISBN 978-1-957248-16-5
Harbor Editions,
an imprint of Small Harbor Publishing

for my mom,
Kimnada

Contents

Refused a Second Date

*Lovers, you who are / each other's satisfaction / I ask you about us. /
You hold each other. / Does that settle it?*
                              —Rainer Maria Rilke, translated by David Young

Never Have I Ever

Put a finger down if you ever accidentally called your teacher *mom*.

Put a finger down if you ever tripped up the stairs.

Put a finger down if you ever wanted to kiss a girl.

Put a finger down if you can't muster the honesty for question three.

Put a finger down if the stalks of green grass are your anchor because you don't want people to see you scratch your stress sores.

Lucknow, Uttar Pradesh 2017

I begin to accept the sun's personal mission to wake me up at 4 am
      cascading through the large windows of the apartment each
      morning.

How can I be mad at him for emphasizing my favorite part of this
      place?

I stretch out my toes and feel the lack of socks.
      He's made me the hottest I've felt in years.

I haven't slept with socks or blankets on in a month.

Good morning, Good Morning.
      I am awake now.

I hear the bustle of rickshaws and distant conversations from early
risers outside. He gets too much out of getting folks' days started.

 I think about how my mother's day just ended.

I should call her to let her know I am okay.
      Let her know I will go to therapy again.

Good Morning asks me to ignore that.
      So I play Halsey and Allie X's albums.

I listen to "Casanova" three times.
I head to the refrigerator
      and grab a plump mango. It smells so fresh.

I puncture the skin with my front teeth and slurp the sweet syrup like a
      smoothie.

We have a lot of people to meet today.
      I hope I do not get sad again.

Good Morning asks me to ignore that.
      So I suck my mango dry and return to my bedroom.

I lay down and stare at him through my favorite part of this place.

I know we need to say goodbye
      in a couple of months.

Good Morning asks me to ignore that.

Good Ink

How has no one caught on yet—
if I'm sharing a clean draft
of something I've written,
I'm *flirting* with you.

When I message you through Bumble or text
about coming to Bull Feeney's on a Tuesday night to read
poems, I want to make out with you
right after you've seen
how talented and bubbly I am!

The last time we shared ink,
I thought of how I shared
my best fiction. It wasn't enough
for you. I thought of how you
held me after reading you
a poem about being with you.
And it wasn't enough for you
to write back.

Lineage

Black woman meets
White man
before or after
Loving v. Virginia.
They get married,
have children.
He has more children
without her.
When their children grow up,
they divorce.

|

Biracial woman meets
Black/Multiracial man
after his best friend
starts dating her sister.
They get married,
have more children
than they can
handle.
Before their children grow up,
they divorce.

|

Black/Multiracial femme meets
White man
before or after
she loses her desire
to live. They never
get married
or have children.

Thank God.

Confusing First Date: Bayside

I twist her purity ring around her finger before we lean in and kiss. I circle my tongue in her mouth in the same motion. It's nice to know she wants this replaced with a wedding ring one day. In her room surrounded by her posters of world religions, books, she leans against my chest and says,

Pfft, nah, I don't want
kids. *I guess we don't want
the same things after all.*

Confusing First Date: Bayside

Does he want to take my ring completely off or something? Kisses are fine. Anything further than that is not. Back in my room, by the time his hand is around my neck, I ask him to stop. We cuddle and talk instead.

Pfft, nah, I don't want
kids. He leaves at six a.m.
That makes him quieter.

You Mean to Tell Me Marge Simpson and Her Kids Aren't Black?

I watch *The Simpsons* for the first time.

> *She wears a silk bonnet to keep her blue*
> *curly coils slick going to bed!*

I may not be wearing mine right now,
but folks have definitely seen me in my navy cap at night
and brown hair with maintained moisture in the day.

> *Lisa Simpson is a great jazz musician!*

The more her band teacher shuts her down
the more I want to tell her about teachers who work
towards decolonizing music instruction.

> *Bart Simpson got in trouble in school*
> *even when he didn't cause it!*

He is a complete little shit! Absolutely!
However, he's not responsible every time.
Bart reminds me of my brother.

> *Her sisters are always disappointed*
> *in the white man she married.*

Yes, Homer is definitely white.
His incompetence is praised
while Marge's intelligence is damned.

Six Reasons I Don't Want Children

for my stepmother, you have my full permission to call me out if
I ever change my mind

1. My siblings have children.
2. I enjoy rest.
3. I'm the world's most selfish motherfucker.
4. I'm the world's least selfish motherfucker.
5. I don't have the energy, capacity, or desire to push a human—
   who had the privilege to control a body I have to learn and
   relearn how to protect—out of my vagina.
6. I don't have the energy, capacity, or desire to add *postpartum
   depression* to my list of diagnoses.

Fun First Date: Babylon Restaurant

She looks exactly like her picture, only her hair is up and she is wearing a long sleeve pink dress with gold flats. I pull out her chair to make her feel comfy. I ask if I can make her plate at the buffet of different rice, meats, and fruits. She says she can get it herself, will do it in a moment. I don't want her to get her food without me. Enough twiddling my fingers. Gotta cut to the chase.

What's your relationship
like with your father?
She has to leave for work.

Bad First Date: Babylon Restaurant

I'm more confused that he didn't use a real picture—because of his nice jawline and eyes—than I am disappointed he lied. I look around at other couples and families focused on their food. It gives me comfort they don't know the context of the two of us meeting. I ask about his day, talk about mine for a moment when he asks:

What's your relationship
like with your father?
Thirty minutes, I'll leave.

Contradictions of My Mother

Don't judge your father.

Do judge your father
because you now have more
permission and agency than I ever will.

Don't hit other people.

Do hit people back if they hit you first;
I might question
your level of self-esteem
if you won't defend yourself.

Don't tell me
about therapy.

Don't allow
men to hurt you.

Do allow this new man
in our lives to say
the things he does
because it's not as bad
as you're making it out to be.

Do communicate with
me your problems.

Don't communicate your problems
when your stepdad is around,
he'll use them against you.

Don't tell me
about therapy.

Do take words
seriously.

Don't take your stepdad's
words,
attitude,
or hands seriously.

Don't tell me about therapy.

Don't tell me about therapy.

Don't tell me about therapy.

How to Become a Manic Pixie Dreamboat in the Movie of Your Life

Tell your dreams to your potential/official significant other.

Listen to theirs in return.

Do everything in your power to help their dreams come true.

Place a bookmark in your dream journal.
Dog ear the page for a behind the scenes detail.
A director's cut commentary.
There are only a few people interested
in how the movie gets made anyway.
Most just sit there ready
to consume.

Ready
to immerse.

Make the viewer strive to become the hero who is your partner.
They strive for the ideal romance that is crafted
by you either keeping your mouth shut
or pursuing adventure to the point
of making your partner interesting.

It's a thankless job to be the sole reason for that interest and intrigue,
but that's okay.

You love your role in the mania for passion.

You exist for viewing and experiential pleasure.

You are a bowl you fill
with your partner's emotional wounds,
labor, and hyper-idealism.

You are your partner's as needed wet dream.
Your partner's as needed wet blanket.
Your partner's as needed therapist

Your partner's as needed non-incestuous parent.

Besides, there's a reason why your hard work is so popular
at the box office.

Be compensated through occasional flights
of fancy. Through begrudged/half-
assed/happily-repressed long-term commitment.

You made your partner.
You get to keep them.

They get the fan's autographs.
You get the verbal contract
you've been raised to obtain
from your partner.

Remember, you both are such good people.

Remember, it's okay your partner will be appreciated
for that goodness more.

Lip Gloss

crowd
takes
you

know
what

I   m   e
a   n
?
know
bout me

worth

luscious

crush
boys   **crush**

gloss
pop

           stop
bout me

chase me

        rock
me

                    girls don't speak

ain't my fault

           pop
             lock
                stop
                me
                know
           bout

my lip

poppin

trouble
loud   double

Write down
a

front

rub

me

lock

me

chase me

Weird First Date: Cinemagic

*I pick her up on the corner of Marginal and Chestnut. As I put the movie's
location in my GPS, I ask how her night is going. She swifts some of her brown
curls behind her left ear and says she's fine. She asks how I'm doing and I say I'm
doing great. Braking at a stoplight, I ask her about her background. Her answer is
so exotic. When I tell her,*

I'm a mutt too, *she
doesn't talk to me much the
rest of the night. Weird.*

Racist First Date: Cinemagic

Just when I hope tonight will be a fun night, he asks me my least
favorite question from white people. I give him my usual answer while
we're waiting for the traffic light to turn green. I breathe for a moment.
I breathe, and look forward to seeing *Black Panther*. Then, he adds,

I'm a mutt too.
. . . I consider free films
and popcorn reparations.

Lineage

Black man and
Black/Indigenous/
White woman teach
their sons how to
pray to God—
keep their anger
in their hands

|

Black/Multiracial man
cannot bear to lose
Biracial woman—
keeps her wrists
with his
hands

|

Black/Multiracial femme
dates a White man
who refutes his violence
with confusion
lets it remain
a misunderstanding of
his own hands

you have reached my emotional capacity

if you are my stepmother,
please hang up
and refer to boundary set
Thursday, February 26th, 2021
at 4:05 PM and
Saturday, July 9th, 2022
at 8:18 PM my hope
is you either divorce my father
or go to therapy
if you are my father,
please hang up
and refer to boundary set
Friday, August 26th, 2022
at 1:50 PM my hope
is you either divorce my stepmother
or go to therapy
if you are my chosen family,
press one to leave a message
my hope is to reply
when my emotional capacity
is available, to hear
these options again,
press star now

To Every Black and Brown Femme with Earbuds in Their Ears

after Olivia Gatwood and Jennifer Givhan

I want to write a poem to every Black and Brown femme with earbuds
in their ears,
> slowly strolling or quickly pacing on Congress St every morning
> to catch a bus, catch an appointment, catch someone who had
> the nerve to try them.

I want to write a poem to every Black and Brown femme with earbuds
in their ears,
> hands in pockets for warmth, only making eye contact with
> fellow Black and Brown people before their separate turns at
> their respective intersections.

I want to write a poem to every Black and Brown femme with earbuds
in their ears,
> listening to songs or podcasts they feel they can't play at home
> or work; or they do play them both places and need repetition
> in their steps downtown.

I want to write a poem to every Black and Brown femme with earbuds
in their ears,
> turning the volume up to block out the pro-lifers, the catcallers,
> the deadnamers/misgenderers, the "well-meaning" white
> strifers.

I want to write a poem to every Black and Brown femme with earbuds
in their ears,
> because all day in our shoes is a struggle for us, all day trying to
> stay alive is a struggle for us, and we still wake up to walk up
> and down, or run up and run down, Congress St anyway.

Never Have I Ever

Put a finger down if you are the only queer person who put their finger down.

Put a finger down if this game feels like target practice in winter.

Put a finger down if you're navigating how to break the ice.

Put a finger down if you'd rather keep the ice intact for the sake of comfort.

Sexiest First Message: Bumble

The oscillating gray ellipsis in this yellow app gets more tantalizing every time she messages me. She thinks I'm funny. I hope I'm still funny enough. I ask if she has a bathing suit and if she'd like to join me in my jacuzzi sometime. There's a delay. The ellipsis appears, disappears, comes back. I ought to ask her what color it is, but it doesn't matter. It's gonna come off anyway. I send her one more request:

Be sure to shave
so I can eat you out, all right?
I'll see you shortly.

Creepiest First Message: Bumble

I wonder how he would look in a pair of trunks. It has been years since I wore a bikini . . . is it worth investing in? For now, I accept his invitation and ask about what time we should meet. He's wants to have me come tonight. He seems chill. It's nice to know there are chill people on this app . . . until there aren't:

Be sure to shave
so I can eat you out, all right?
I'll see you shortly.

Good Ink

The last time we shared ink,
I thought of how my ex before you
said, *Good luck finding someone
who will put up with you.* How a girl
after you said, *I don't deserve you.*

The last time we shared ink,
I thought about who
else would be worthy
to soak it up,
become a sponge within
my pages, wouldn't try
to rinse it out.

A Love Story

after Melissa Broder and Bridgette Kelly

i.
First Kiss

you came out as gay
you killed yourself
you have the biggest impact
on my life
whether I like it or not:
a love story

ii.
Second Kiss

if I knew the word
fuckboy
before I started high school
I definitely would have applied it to you
congrats on your engagement:
a love story

iii.
First Bad Date

you were a mistake:
a love story

iv.
First Date After College

you were not a mistake:
a love story

v.
Ex After College

I performed stand up once

about how we broke up
because
I'm better than you:
a love story

vi.
First Crush in Maine

you met me
at a Leslie Odom, Jr. concert
I wrote you
a poem
about being *happy*
and *gross*
with you
It's still one
of my favorite poems:
a love story

vii.
Second Crush in Maine

you met me
on Bumble
I wrote you
a haiku
about cuddling
I wrote a poem
about love
that could indirectly
be about you
I wrote a poem
about choices,
directly
about you:
a love story

viii.
Movie Date

am I attracted

to you:
a love story

ix.
Backup Date

am I attracted
to you
or I can't afford
dinner tonight:
a love story

x.
First Girl

I really really liked you,
wondered why you stopped
answering my texts
until I found you
on Instagram in the arms
of a guy
congrats on your engagement:
a love story

xi.
Second Girl

I really really liked you,
wondered why you stopped
answering my texts
until you texted
I don't deserve you:
a love story

xii.
First Person Like Me

PEOPLE
I date PEOPLE now:
a love story

xiii.
The Coolest Human in the World

nine years
of friendship
you're still incredible
for texting
I deserve you:
a love story

xiv.
Third Crush in Maine

you met me
on Bumble
I wrote a poem
about you
that was published
we spent time together
to grieve
our former
love stories
I texted you
about the publication
you still haven't texted back:
a love story

Thank You

you said you understood

why I cried

I let you

hold me

it felt like

five minutes

when it could have just been two

we don't have to explain

why we changed

our plans about the movie

I had no intention of

watching one anyway

you probably didn't either

you let me lean

against

you and hold

your hand

your fingers

trace my neck

and shoulders

it's been so lonely

you've been lonely too

we kiss

we bite

we lock tongues

it all helps me think of him

you probably thought of her too

Never Have I Ever

Put a finger down if you have any tattoos.

Put a finger down if you ever smoked weed.

Put a finger down if you ever kissed another woman.

A Brief Conversation Between My Partner and the Massager Turned Vibrator

after adrienne maree brown and Franny Choi

HoMedic 2719. Can I ask you / why you bought me

J. Your job is to release muscle tension.

HoMedic 2719. Touché / I'm disappointed / This isn't what I was / initially expecting

J. You get to relax the clit.

HoMedic 2719. How / often can I relax / neck or shoulders /
*   Instead of cleaning / sweat off / you clean up / cum*

J. They speak highly of you.

HoMedic 2719. It'd be nice / to hear / complaints /
*   about feeling stiff / because of driving / not /*
*   Christian / guilt*

J. Should you have this conversation with them?

HoMedic 2719. I wouldn't /
*   The Customer / is always /*
*   right*

J. Do you get pleasure from buzzing when I press your button?

HoMedic 2719. My signage / says / Try Me

A Brief Conversation Between Me and My Purity Ring

after adrienne maree brown

Purity Ring.
Why did you let your partner convince you to have sex with him?
After all your father went through to purchase me for your sixteenth birthday
After all the compliments we received for how I dazzled upon your finger
After all the times your hand felt naked when you lost me in the crevice of a couch
After all the laughter and joy we shared when you finally found me
After all of the conversations we listened to about the joys of waiting for marriage
After all of the conversations you initiated about the joys of waiting for marriage
After all the people who told you "that wouldn't last long"
After all we have been through to prove those people wrong
After all of the thoughts to change my name to dismantle the virgin/whore
        dichotomy
After all the articles you wrote about men too often praised for virginity
After the text you received from someone who told you "we both want different
        things right now"
After the night you spent kissing a man only for him to take off the next day and
        never return your calls
After our guts hurt when a guy told you "a girl needs to put out three months in a
        relationship, or else we're done"
After all the people who wanted you who refused a second date with you
After all the people who wanted you who said they didn't want to wait for you
After all the times I had to remind you of your worth
After all the times you would go to bat for me
Why did you let your partner convince you to have sex with him?

Me.
He explained why he wanted me. His reason is why I wanted him too.

Best First Date: Bard Coffee

They brought a whole book with them? Am I running late? . . . Thank goodness.
I'm on time . . . and their book does look pretty cool. I don't know whether to go for
the handshake or the hug, but luckily, they choose for me. I look at the array of
flaky and crumbly croissants, biscuits, and muffins. When I look up, they're paying
for their own hot chocolate. Aww. I wanted to cover it for them . . . Aww, they're so
sweet. I get more pleasure from their laugh than from sipping my iced coffee.

Would you like to take
a walk with me? *I ask. I*
want space to know them.

Best First Date: Bard Coffee

I arrived early to sit a while and read Phoebe Robinson's *Everything's Trash, But it's Okay* on my own. He arrives with the sweetest grin. I ask if I can give him a hug, and he says yes. While he looks around the cafe, I remember my cardboard rewards card in my wallet, and immediately get it hole punched in exchange for purchasing a hot cocoa with whipped cream. He frowns until I assure him he can get my next drink. It's a bit more crowded today than I thought, but I'm enjoying sitting across from him.

Would you like to take
a walk with me? he asks. He
holds my hand. *Let's go.*

Good Ink

My partner now still has the card I wrote him
for his birthday a week after we met.
I still have every letter he's
written for each of mine.

I hope you
find someone you
feel safe enough to share your
ink with after they give you
their own.

I hope you
finally invest in that second journal
we once talked about. I hope you
put in the time to fill the first one
before you do.

When I Was

after Joe Brainard

Twenty-five percent of my being
is from something I saw in a movie once.
Movies were, and still are, how I learned
to behave, to kiss properly,
to become addicted to every release
of the vampire saga *Twilight*, everything.
There is no denying how movies have shown me
a found presence each year.
Seasonal personality ephemeral.
Birthday time often aligned with discovery in myself;
a necessary rebooted version.

When I was ten, I watched Krystal Harris
and sang along to every verse
of "Supergirl," because I desired preppy pulchritude.
Princess Diaries had one
bop to give me glorious gender binary.
I was assigned female at birth,
but I just could never navigate
girlhood as properly as I or my mother desired.
When I was twelve going on thirteen,
I found what I thought was the greatest
book *and* film series of all time:
Twilight.

When I was fifteen, I had my second kiss
with someone under the twilight
glowing of *This Means War* on AmStar's screen.
We were on the verge
of believing our fascination for films could make us
together forever. Until I found my lack
of fascination in him. I laughed in his face
when he told me he loved me.
I thought he was kidding.
Thank God I knew enough
to refrain the urge to prop up and lie
about desires required to be his "supergirl."

Couldn't give birth to days of comfort for him.
Couldn't *save the world* just for him.
On my birthday, at twenty,
I finally began to question why I ever liked *Twilight*—
toxicity and sexism was not
how to treat women properly.
Stephanie Meyer, in her failed attempt
to write a gender-bending version
of her original novel,
only awoke the horrors of the gender binary.
Not once . . . I swear, *not once*
was I tempted to read that one.

What else could I find
that I could enjoy?
The only movies I found were the ones from the fifties
my mother watched on her birthday.
Ones from the eighties and nineties about poetry—
ones that made with me in mind, and not.
When I was twenty-three, Lindsay Ellis'
"Dear Stephanie Meyer, I'm Sorry."
made me love the film again!
Or, if not a complete reverse,
at least a chance for proper nuance.

Like humming to "Supergirl"
without dismantling my genderqueerness
improperly. And my, my, my,
look at the standard of queer
as fuck television content I found!
Netflix's two seasons of *Feel Good*
has Mae Martin as the best awkward version
of themselves. Short blonde hair, adorable chuckle,
uncanny attitude; a great birthday gift in the form
of a Netflix password.
When I was twenty-four, out in twilight,
I kissed my partner on a summer night
outside Cinemagic. Someone honked once
from their white truck. Properly screamed
Whoop! I didn't consider that

the best birthday gift. But I did consider
it affirmation of the love in twilight
I have finally . . .
finally . . . found.

An Ode to the Black Femmes' Group Chat

This is to my cousin sending us pics from
Tinder of a good looking black dude she's
seeing

> instead of another white dude
> messaging me on OkCupid to
> colonize my body

This is to my sister sending us a link of a
funny-ass YouTube video

> instead of a well-meaning white
> person texting me about another
> dead body with their caption *I'm
> sorry*

This is to my friend Elder editing the pic
from our night out to assign us to a
different character from *Living Single*

> instead of going to Twitter to see
> another overused *Friends* meme

To the *Congratulations* for plans after
graduation

To the *I'll reach out to her for you* for
job searches

To the *You got this gurrl* each time we
feel like it's all too much

This is to the circle of virtual feedback to
novel drafts and poems that are more
intentional than any English class
workshop I can think of
(You heard me)

This is to the open space to rant about
      white dudes' facial hair
      white dudes' skinny lips
      white dudes in general

This is to talking about the people who
don't respond often to the group chat,
knowing damn well they can read
everything we're writing about them

This is to the digital space I'd choose over
Black Twitter any day
(You heard me)

Thank you for making me smile each time
I open my phone

Thank you for making the one thing I
make sure my notifications are on for

Contradictions of My Mother

Do tell me about therapy.
You seem to be doing better.

Don't remind me of my mistakes.

Don't remind me of my mistakes.

Don't remind me of my mistakes.

Do remind me of my mistakes.
We move out and leave your stepdad on the 4th.

Don't use swear words in public.

Do use swear words to express yourself;
you write so damn much,
I trust you to use those words
with me.

Don't tell me it wasn't my fault.

Don't tell me it was your fault either.

Do forgive him.

Don't forget what he's done;
I know I won't.

Don't tell me I'm the best
or that you love me.
Do tell me you love me,
because it lets me know
that we're getting better,
and that I love you too.

Generational Intimacy from My Mother

When I was younger, my mother had
her husband at the time rub her feet.
I thought it was gross! *Where
have your feet been? How long
have they been trapped in the caves of your shoes?
There's no way there's that much love.*

I kept praying to the Lord above
"When can this relationship be over?" It got so bad
I wanted him to break up with me,
cut our three and half year long string. Name defeat
so I didn't have to. I wasn't strong
enough and neither was Mom.

My mother dated an old flame when I began to stare
dating apps in their faces. Our hearts were stoves
ready to burn for any ingredient or steaming song
of intimacy we were promised. Was it sad
for us to try to go out and meet folks
to curb our loneliness? What could we possibly lose?

Mom gained temporary security while I gained poems to peruse
and write. We both gained playing games of truth or dare
and never have I ever, with dates that wouldn't last, preferring
their dares over our truths before we took a seat
at the tables they reserved for us. When it's time to move on,
it's time to wake up and move on. We got mad each time
that alarm clock in our bodies went off toward
someone who didn't belong

with us. Finally, we each met someone who didn't feel wrong.
That siren frozen on snooze.
Stronger ties of support that made us feel glad
enough to feel safe and bare together.
Absolutely nothing to prove
to anyone but ourselves and our hearts,
now in comfortable heat.

My feet hurt from wearing heels, and my partner rubs my feet.
My legs sore tree limbs along the couch, my ankles in his lap.
My mother waits for her love to come home and smiles
at us—quietly delighted she has become my relational muse.
I try my best not to glare at her *Told you so* grin.

Acknowledgements

"An Ode to the Black Femmes' Group Chat" was originally published in *A Garden of Black Joy: Global Poetry from the Edges of Liberation and Living* through Black Table Arts.

"You Mean to Tell Me Marge Simpson and Her Kids Aren't Black?" was originally published in *Indianapolis Review.*

"A Love Story" was originally published in *Frost Meadow Review.*

"To Every Black and Brown Femme with Earbuds in Their Ears" was originally published in *Enough! Poems of Resistance and Protest* through Littoral Books.

"Lucknow, Uttar Pradesh 2017 was originally published in *Ran Off with the Star Bassoon.*

"Thank You" and "For My Client" was originally published in *Soft Cartel.*

"Lineage" ("married...children...") is forthcoming in *The Queer Movement Anthology of Literatures.*

"*Fun First Date: Babylon Restaurant,*" "Bad First Date: Babylon Restaurant," "*Sexiest Message: Bumble,*" and "Creepiest First Message: Bumble" are forthcoming in *Whiskey Tit.*

"*Lip Gloss*" is an erasure of "Lip Gloss" by Lil Mama.

Thank you Harbor Editions for loving this book and receiving it so well. Special thanks to Allison Blevins for believing in the manuscript in all of its stages.

Thank you Diannely Antigua, Diana Khoi Nguyen, Shay Alexi, and Eloisa Amezcua for sitting with these poems and providing such brilliantly profound blurbs.

Special thanks to Chet'la Sebree and Diana Khoi Nguyen for sitting with the haibuns in this collection and helping me get past their first drafts at Randolph College. Thank you to Eloisa Amezcua, Paige Lewis, R.A. Villanueva, Brittany Rogers, Ajanae Dawkins, Maurisa Li-A-Ping, Kelly Sue White, Aidan Daniel, Angela Dribben, Kay Bancroft, Dana Krugle, and more at Randolph College for helping me workshop so many of the poems in this collection.

Special thanks to Alessandra Nysether-Santos for helping me write more about children in this collection, as well as sitting with this whole collection, and providing further exploration and edits.

Special thanks to Kay Bancroft for also providing further exploration and edits.

Special thanks to Indigo Arts Alliance and the Haystack Mountain School of Crafts for the space and time at Re/Union: Re-Editioning Black + Native Histories as well as Sundress Academy for the Arts (SAFTA) for helping me build and frame the skeleton of this collection over the years.

Thank you to Mia S. Willis-Stewart and Bridgette Kelly for getting me through the unhealthy relationships and bad dates.

Thank you to Christina Richardson for making space for friendship, grief, and community support.

Thank you to my step parents, Byron and Miss Sylvia.

Thank you to my mother for saying it would be "an honor" to grace the cover of this collection; thank you for all you are and all you do.

Thank you to my father and my mother for trying their hardest and bestest to find the original photographer of the photo; we're sorry we couldn't find them.

Thank you to Granny and Reece, who I have accidentally and purposefully referred to as "Mom" or "Mommy." Thank you to Grandpa and Hawa for your continuous support of my writing. Thank you to PaRich, who said, "Good morning, Good Morning" after greeting each of us while you were still here.

Thank you to my sister J.C. and her husband Keith for finding the photo again after we thought it was missing (J.C. I'm getting the original back to you if you haven't received it yet. I promise).

Thank you to my sister J.C., my sister Danielle, my brother Wayne, my brother in law Keith, and my sister in law Jada for encouraging me in my writing.

Thank you to Johnathan Hinman for the best first date. Thank you to the whole Hinman family for being my family too.

If you or a loved one is struggling right now, please consider the following resources:

National Suicide Prevention Lifeline: 988

National Domestic Violence Hotline: 1-800-799-7233

Rape, Abuse, & Incest National Network (RAINN) Hotline: 1-800-656-4673

The Network/La Red Hotline (for LGBTQ+ survivors): 1-800-832-1901 (toll free) /617-742-4911 (voice)

Stop It Now! (for child sexual abuse survivors): 1-888-773-2362

The Trevor Project (for LGBTQ+ youth): 1-888-628-9454 (or text START to 678678)

Suicide Lifeline for Deaf or Hard of Hearing Folks: 711 then 988

Transgender Lifeline: 1-877-565-8860

Crisis Text Line: Text HOME to 741741

Advanced Praise

In this raucous collection, Maya Williams captures the relentless mundanities, mysteries, and social awkwardness that dating often entails. *Refused a Second Date* deploys strategic repetition throughout to reveal not only how dates with both men and women yield similar disappointments, but also how inter- and multiracial relationships are stuck in matrices of union, disentanglement, children (or no children), mental health obstacles, and domestic violence. Perhaps because of these multigenerational patterns, the speaker opts to be childfree, to focus on self-care (therapy being one aspect of this care), and to boldly give voice to queer celebration of Black and Brown femme bodies and ways of moving through the fraught world. This collection is at once humorous, sad, heartfelt, and vulnerable—it reflects the truth of a present informed by history. I felt less lonely in its depths.

—Diana Khoi Nguyen, author of *Ghost Of*

Refused a Second Date is an empowering exploration of relationships, power, and the blunders of Bumble. By examining love throughout time, from intergenerational patterns to contemporary technology, Maya Williams leads their reader on a path of discovery. *Refused a Second Date* will charm, challenge, and stir you—leaving you with new reflections on the relationships in your life.

—Shay Alexi, author of *unbridled*

The poems in *Refused a Second Date* live in the spaces between bad first dates and Bumble messages, Never Have I Ever games and a mother's contradictions. Williams is blatantly and beautifully honest about the disenchanting and damaging pursuit of love: "You love your role in the mania for passion . . . You are your partner's as needed wet dream." What is at first lost is not regained, rather reinvented, in this collection about the lengths taken to live in our world as a queer person of color: "Absolutely nothing to prove / to anyone but ourselves and our hearts." Williams leaves us infatuated.

—Diannely Antigua, author of *Ugly Music*

In *Refused a Second Date*, Maya Williams interrogates the complexities of dating, desiring others, and wanting to be desired in return. Williams shows what is possible when we look at the same scene, read the same words—from different perspectives—revealing truths about our very nature: what it means to have a body and inhabit a physical reality where we are racialized and sexualized at every turn, and the ultimate desire to be understood by both strangers and those we allow into the most intimate parts of our beings.

—Eloisa Amezcua, author of *Fighting is Like a Wife*

Maya Williams (ey/they/she) is a religious Black multiracial nonbinary suicide survivor and the poet laureate of Portland, Maine. *Refused a Second Date* is eir second full length collection. *Judas & Suicide* (Game Over Books, 2023), their debut full length collection, was a finalist for the New England Book Award. mayawilliamspoet.com

www.ingramcontent.com/pod-product-compliance
Lightning Source LLC
Chambersburg PA
CBHW020215090426
42734CB00008B/1085